CELEBRATING THE FAMILY NAME OF RAMÍREZ

Celebrating the Family Name of Ramírez

Walter the Educator

Silent King Books
a WhichHead Entertainment Imprint

Copyright © 2024 by Walter the Educator

All rights reserved. No part of this book may be reproduced in any manner whatsoever without written permission except in the case of brief quotations embodied in critical articles and reviews.

First Printing, 2024

Disclaimer

This book is a literary work; the story is not about specific persons, locations, situations, and/or circumstances unless mentioned in a historical context. Any resemblance to real persons, locations, situations, and/or circumstances is coincidental. This book is for entertainment and informational purposes only. The author and publisher offer this information without warranties expressed or implied. No matter the grounds, neither the author nor the publisher will be accountable for any losses, injuries, or other damages caused by the reader's use of this book. The use of this book acknowledges an understanding and acceptance of this disclaimer.

Celebrating the Family Name of Ramírez is a memory book that belongs to the Celebrating Family Name Book Series by Walter the Educator. Collect them all and more books at WaltertheEducator.com

USE THE EXTRA SPACE TO DOCUMENT YOUR FAMILY MEMORIES THROUGHOUT THE YEARS

RAMÍREZ

In lands where ancient rivers flow,

Celebrating the Family Name of

Ramírez

And mountains wear their winter snow,

The name Ramírez proudly stands,

A legacy across the lands.

From distant shores to desert plains,

Where sun and shadow share domains,

The Ramírez name has carved its way,

A tale of courage, night and day.

With every dawn, the story starts,

In beating drums, in beating hearts,

The Ramírez spirit fierce and bright,

Guides us through the darkest night.

Their roots run deep in fertile ground,

In every breeze, their whispers sound,

Of dreams pursued and battles won,

Of endless toil beneath the sun.

Celebrating the Family Name of

Ramírez

In every child, a fire burns,

A passion that the world returns,

The Ramírez name, a guiding star,

A light that shines from near to far.

Through valleys deep and forests wide,

Wherever Ramírez may abide,

They bring with them a warmth, a grace,

That no one else could quite replace.

The winds may howl, the storms may rage,

But Ramírez turns each page,

With wisdom gained from years before,

They chart a course, they seek the shore.

In every laugh, in every tear,

The Ramírez name is held so dear,

A tapestry of love and life,

Celebrating the Family Name of

Ramírez

Of joy and sorrow, peace and strife.

Their hands have built, their hearts have healed,

In every field, the truth revealed,

That Ramírez walks a path of pride,

With every step, they do not hide.

The name Ramírez, a melody,

Of unity and harmony,

In every voice, in every song,

Celebrating the Family Name of

Ramírez

They carry forth the dream so strong.

ABOUT THE CREATOR

Walter the Educator is one of the pseudonyms for Walter Anderson. Formally educated in Chemistry, Business, and Education, he is an educator, an author, a diverse entrepreneur, and he is the son of a disabled war veteran. "Walter the Educator" shares his time between educating and creating. He holds interests and owns several creative projects that entertain, enlighten, enhance, and educate, hoping to inspire and motivate you. Follow, find new works, and stay up to date with Walter the Educator™

at WaltertheEducator.com

www.ingramcontent.com/pod-product-compliance
Lightning Source LLC
LaVergne TN
LVHW012052070526
838201LV00082B/3920